Written by Matthew Needler and Phil Southam (FyreUK). All rights reserved.
Edited by Stephanie Milton.
Designed by Andrea Philpots, Matthew Garrett, and Joe Bolder.
Builds created by Matthew Needler and Phil Southam (FyreUK), salmon77,
halfdemonanbu, Sir_Beret, Geroo, Nefashus, Heaven_Lord, CrespoChimp, iHDVibeZz.
Illustrations by James Barker, Joe Bolder, and Theo Cordner.
Production by Louis Harvey and Caroline Hancock.
Special thanks to Lydia Winters, Owen Hill, and Junkboy.

MOJANG

Published by arrangement with Mojang and Egmont®

ISBN 978-0-545-82321-0

10 9 8 7 6 5 4 3 2   16 17 18 19/0

Printed in China   38
First published 2014
This edition first printing 2015

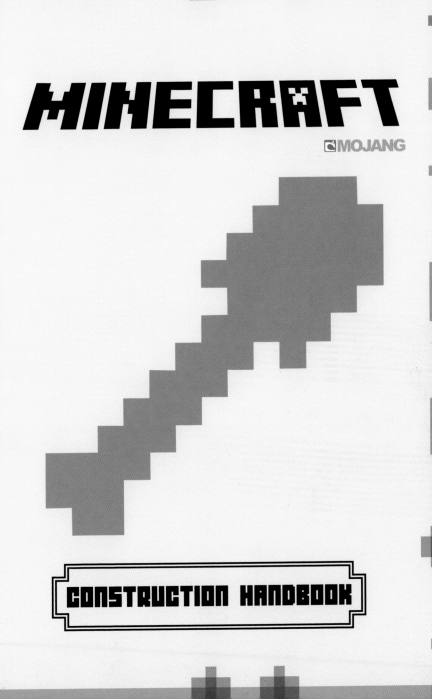

MINECRAFT

CONSTRUCTION HANDBOOK

CONTENTS

INTRODUCTION

WELCOME TO THE OFFICIAL MINECRAFT CONSTRUCTION HANDBOOK! IT'S ESSENTIAL READING FOR ASPIRING MASTER BUILDERS.

It contains step-by-step instructions from expert builders FyreUK to help you complete awesome constructions, plus examples of inspirational builds to get you thinking big.

Whether you dream of building your own mansion with a stunning garden or love the thrill of a bone-rattling roller-coaster ride, this handbook will give you the confidence and skills to attempt some of those big projects that have just been pipe dreams up until now.

So let's get building!

TIP: STAYING SAFE ONLINE

Playing Minecraft on multiplayer servers is a lot of fun! Here are a few simple rules to help you stay safe and keep the world of Minecraft a great place to spend time:

- Never give out your real name — don't use it as your username.
- Never give out any of your personal details.
- Never tell anybody which school you go to or how old you are.
- Never tell anybody your password except a parent or guardian.

WOODEN HOUSE

You may need to build a house to protect yourself and your possessions in Survival mode, or you might want to build a beautiful village in Creative mode. Whatever your requirements, houses are one of the most important constructions to get right.

CONSTRUCTION MATERIALS

1

First, create a simple 1-block-tall outline using cobblestone blocks. Add a slight outcrop at the front for an entrance and a slight dip at the back for a rear porch.

2

Build up the first-floor walls bearing in mind how high you'd like your ceiling to be. We'd recommend at least 1 or 2 blocks of space above your head so it doesn't feel too cramped. Fill in your ground floor using wood planks.

3

Build up the second-floor walls in wood planks to complement the cobblestone. It's often easier to fill in the entire wall, then knock any excess blocks out to add windows. Add in your first floor using wood planks followed by a handy wooden staircase.

4

DOOR RECIPE

You can craft 3 wooden doors from 6 planks of the same type of wood.

Use glass blocks to create windows and wood blocks to define the edges of your house. Add 2 sets of wooden double doors to the entrance and torches to light it all up at night. Finally, lay out your rooms and decorate your house.

WOODEN HOUSE ...CONTINUED

CONSTRUCTION MATERIALS

 TIP: You'll need to place a stair block next to a regular block, then destroy the regular block once the stair is in position. Aim for the lower half of the block you're placing them against so they're placed in an upward direction. If you aim for the upper part of a block, the stairs will face downward.

5

Extend the front of the house upward in a triangle shape using wood planks. Then use wood stair blocks to create the edge of the triangle shape of the roof.

6

Fill in your roof so that it covers the entire entrance section. Overhanging eaves will really make your house stand out, so extend the roof 1 block forward, too.

WOOD STAIR RECIPE

4

You can craft 4 wood stair blocks from 6 wood planks.

 Stair blocks placed at 90-degree angles to each other will form a corner.

7

Continue to add wood stair blocks in rows as shown until you've created a roof for the rest of the house.

8

Once your house is completely covered, remember to add a 1-block overhang to each section of the roof.

FINISHING TOUCHES

Try adding balconies, a window in the roof, and a cobblestone chimney. If you want to give the impression that smoke is billowing out of your chimney, place several cobwebs above it. The building techniques used for this house can be applied to more complex builds. Try them out on different house designs, and check out some of the impressive cities built by the Minecraft community for more inspiration.

CHATEAU DE RESQUER
BY SALMON77

Minecrafter salmon77 created this elaborate house on an isolated island using a combination of sandstone and wood. It's a perfect second project after you've mastered building a basic home.

The natural landscape is used to its best advantage, making use of most of the island and following the natural shape of the land, as well as retaining several trees and small grassy areas around the house. This approach would also work well for houses built on hillsides or mountains.

The dramatic staircase leading up to the entrance is particularly grand. This impressive feature is made from a variety of complementary blocks and immediately draws the eye.

TIPS TO TAKE FROM THIS BUILD:

Work with the natural landscape to create a truly unique design, and for maximum impact build an impressive, raised entrance.

NORDIC HALL BY FYREUK

This large, complex house was created by build team FyreUK. It was constructed using the darkest type of wood available — spruce wood — which contrasts sharply with the snowy landscape.

Nordic Hall is constructed from a mix of raw and refined wood on a cobblestone base. It uses similar principles as the house on page 8 and many of the same details, such as the triangular roof and large windows. But Nordic Hall is built on an entirely different scale — it's 115 blocks tall!

This house was a team effort — a large group of builders worked together to create this detailed, large-scale structure. It would probably take days for someone to replicate this on his or her own.

TIPS TO TAKE FROM THIS BUILD:

For large, ambitious builds, consider working with a team to spread the load and get things finished more quickly.

DECORATIVE GARDEN

Let's work on making your house more homey from the outside. Creating a peaceful, enclosed garden allows you to enjoy the landscape around you in a safe environment.

CONSTRUCTION MATERIALS

1

First, mark the edges of your garden by placing wood blocks in the ground. Choose a spot for your swimming pool, then dig an area 1 block deep and use stone blocks to mark out the edges.

2

Now place leaves on top of your wood blocks (they won't decay if they're placed on wood). Dig your pool to the desired depth and use smooth sandstone and glowstone to line the walls.

3

Once the pool walls are finished, you can fill it with water. Try adding a few more details to your garden at this stage, such as a small vegetable patch and some trees.

4

Fix trapdoors onto dirt blocks to create stylish planters for your flowers. Craft a deck from wood planks, stair blocks, and fences, then place an anvil on top for the barbecue.

ANVIL RECIPE

You can craft an anvil from 4 iron ingots and 3 blocks of iron (made from 9 iron ingots).

TRAPDOOR RECIPE

2

You can craft 2 trapdoors from 6 wood planks of the same type.

DECORATIVE GARDEN
...CONTINUED

Now that you've mastered the basic garden layout, check out these advanced decorative features to take your outside space to the next level. You'll be the envy of the street in no time!

FOUNTAIN

A fountain is a great way to enhance your garden. Fountains may look like they defy the laws of Minecraft, but they're not that hard to make. The trick is to create a structure with an infinite water source at the top that can then fall into an area at the bottom. Once placed, the water will continue to flow indefinitely. You can then create an attractive centerpiece, like this one made from stone bricks and chiseled stone bricks, with a lamp at the top.

CONSTRUCTION MATERIALS

STONE BRICK RECIPE

4

You can craft 4 stone bricks from 4 blocks of smooth stone.

CHISELED STONE BRICK RECIPE

You can craft 1 chiseled stone brick from 2 stone brick slabs.

DID YOU KNOW? An infinite water source can be made by creating a 2x2 square or a 3x1 rectangle of water. Once created, an infinite water source will produce an endless supply of water.

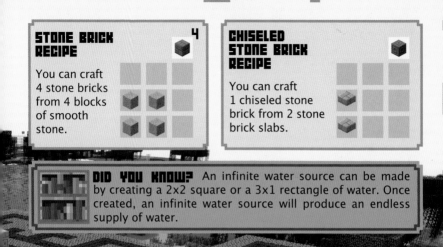

MAZE

One of the most popular uses for leaf blocks is to create mazes. Much like the hedge on page 17, you begin by marking out your maze with wood blocks. When you're happy that your friends will get thoroughly lost in your labyrinth of pathways, place leaf blocks on top of your wood blocks and build them up to 3 or 4 blocks tall so your friends can't jump up and peek over the top.

CONSTRUCTION MATERIALS

STREAM COTTAGE
BY HALFDEMONANBU

This attractive cottage makes great use of the stream running nearby. The random positioning of plants and lily pads has helped create a wild, cabin-in-the-woods feel.

Unlike most gardens, there are no pathways or fences to act as boundaries or guidelines, and no straight lines. The edges are organic and natural. Although the cottage has been built on flat ground, you could build something similar on hilly terrain as well. You can easily create a stream like this one to add a little atmosphere to your garden.

TIPS TO TAKE FROM THIS BUILD:

Well-placed, colorful flowers can transform a simple garden, and lily pads are both functional and attractive.

PALACE GARDENS
BY FYREUK

These magnificent palace gardens are so large that we can't show everything. What you can see here is one of the four corners — an inviting oasis of calm.

TIPS TO TAKE FROM THIS BUILD:

A symmetrical design may seem appropriate for a formal setting, but if you play with asymmetrical designs, you can make a more interesting build.

The pathway is made from a mixture of cobblestone and gravel, and is surrounded by small hedges and greenery. The tree in the center of the garden is planted on a small man-made island with shallow water surrounding it. The island is circular, but it's not quite a perfect circle so it still looks natural and organic.

FORTIFIED WALL

Your towns and cities need to be protected from hostile monsters and enemy players. To ensure the safety of your precious structures, you may want to consider a fortified wall.

CONSTRUCTION MATERIALS

STONE SLAB RECIPE 6

You can craft 6 stone slabs from 3 blocks of smooth stone.

1

First, create the outline of your wall in the block of your choice (we used cobblestone). Decide how many blocks deep you'd like your wall to be. It doesn't matter how long your wall is right now, you can always extend it later if necessary.

2

Build the walls up to the desired height, leaving gaps at regular intervals along the top. These gaps (called crenels) allow archers to fire at your enemies. Add a wood plank walkway to the top of the walls just below the crenels to create battlements.

3

Fortify your wall with another layer. We used stone bricks to build out from the wall and create a pillar-like support system that looks tough to get through. We also added stone brick slabs across the top of the wall to break up the large amount of cobblestone.

4

Add stone brick stairs to the lower section of the wall to allow access from the top of the wall to the bottom. We added corners to each of the pillar sections on the wall, and also added stair blocks above the stone brick running along the middle of the wall.

FORTIFIED WALL
...CONTINUED

Towers placed at each corner of your wall will provide excellent lookout posts. They open up the defensive capabilities of your wall and can be used to access the upper levels.

CONSTRUCTION MATERIALS

1

First, lay out a circular shape at the base of one end of your wall. We used cobblestone so the tower blends in with the rest of the wall.

2

Next, build the tower up to at least double the height of the wall, then add crenels to the top. We blended the wall into the lower section of the tower, but you could build your tower out of a contrasting block.

TIP: If you're feeling especially creative, why not try designing a family/clan shield for your castle wall? Colorful blocks like dyed wool are ideal — they'll really make your shield stand out against the stonework.

3

Time to add some detail. We created two upper layers using stone brick blocks circling the entire tower. This helps break up the large amount of cobblestone. We also added a wood plank walkway to the top of the tower to match the top of the walls.

4

Add windows to each level of your tower by destroying cobblestone blocks in your desired location. Create a staircase inside so that you can easily climb up and down the tower during battle. We also used stone brick stairs to make the two extra layers we added in the previous step appear smoother and extend out a little farther. Finally, we created a torch from netherrack for the top.

DID YOU KNOW? Netherrack is the Nether equivalent of cobblestone. Once set alight it will burn continuously, so it's ideal for torches and fireplaces.

MAGE CITY WALLS BY FYREUK

This circular wall created by FyreUK encloses the mystical Mage City. *Mage* is an old English word for *magician*, and Mage City is a mysterious place, full of magical secrets.

This is a small section of the immense wall that's made up of various layers, with towers at regular intervals.

The entire wall took more than 20 people over 3 hours to create so set aside a few days if you want to try this on your own.

To create a wall of this scale and shape you'd need to make two enormous circles out of blocks: one for the outside of the wall, and one smaller circle for the inside. You'd then need to fill the space between the two circles with blocks — this is an incredibly time-consuming process. And then there are the wall details . . . *phew!*

TIPS TO TAKE FROM THIS BUILD:

Take inspiration from fantasy and run with a theme.

LARGE MEDIEVAL CITY WALL
BY SIR_BERET

Minecrafter Sir_Beret created these elaborate walls to enclose a medieval city. They look impressive enough in pictures, but are even more spectacular up close as they are over 65 blocks tall!

These walls have multiple layers and a suspended walkway on the upper section. Usually you would build your town or city before building your wall, but Sir_Beret decided to build his wall first. He intended to create a city inside, following the shape of the wall, but never got around to it.

TIPS TO TAKE FROM THIS BUILD:

Don't be afraid to create the city to fit the wall, not the other way around.

ROYAL HALL

Have you grown weary of your house? Why not build yourself a royal hall? It'll be a great addition to your Minecraft world. Let's take a look at how you can make your interiors look more regal.

CONSTRUCTION MATERIALS

1

Choose a location for your hall and decide which blocks you'd like to use (we used stone). Mark out a 19-block-wide, 30-block-long, and 10-block-tall outline for your hall. Once the outline is in place, fill in the floor using your chosen block.

2

Mark out areas for windows now, before you fill in the walls. This way it'll be easier to move them if you change your mind. Add a royal carpet down the center of the hall that stops just before the area where your throne will sit. Yes, that's right, you're going to have a throne.

DIFFICULTY ■ ■ □

DID YOU KNOW? Carpet blocks were introduced in the 1.6 update. They are the same thickness as a pressure plate and sit on top of regular blocks. They are also fireproof, which means you don't have to worry about setting the place ablaze. You can craft 15 different colors of carpet.

3

Fill the walls with cobblestone and the windows with glass panes. Add fence blocks with torches on top to light up the room. Now create your throne, making sure it's fit for Minecraft royalty — think gold, diamond, and anything else that might bling it up.

4

Add stone pillars to your throne room for a really authentic touch. The pillars in our example are 2x2 blocks wide and the same height as the walls. We also added a stone brick pattern to the floor to create some detail.

CARPET BLOCK RECIPE

3

You can craft 3 blocks of carpet from 2 wool blocks.

GLASS PANE RECIPE

16

You can craft 16 glass panes from 6 blocks of glass.

DID YOU KNOW?

Diamond blocks can be crafted from 9 diamond gems, and gold blocks from 9 gold ingots. Both of these are an expensive investment, but they make fantastic decorative blocks.

DIAMOND BLOCK RECIPE

Replace the diamonds with gold ingots for a gold block.

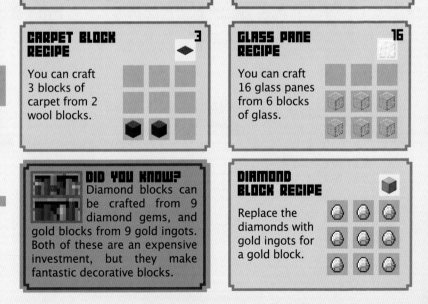

5

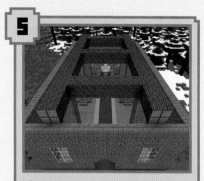

Of course, it's imperative that you keep the rain off your beautiful throne! Add these wood blocks on top of the current stone brick pillars. They'll be the main support for the roof.

6

Next, create the outline shape of the roof using wood planks and stairs, then extend the stair blocks all the way along your royal hall. Add windows at each end to allow natural light in.

TIP: Add a line of wood blocks down the center of the wood plank area of the end wall. You can then use this central line to figure out exactly where to place your windows so that they are symmetrical.

7

Head inside and, using the wood blocks as a reference again, add wooden columns inside the roof. You can also add upside-down stairs for more detail.

8

Run a line of fence blocks across the middle of the roof and add upside-down glowstone lamps. This will provide enough light to stop mobs spawning.

COMMUNITY CREATIONS
THE MOST IMPRESSIVE ROYAL HALLS IN THE KINGDOM!

DWARVEN CITY
BY FYREUK

This hall was made for the fantasy race of the dwarves. The whole build is situated inside a mountain and in places extends down toward the bedrock layer. There's no natural light at all.

Huge cauldrons of lava light up the room, as does the running lava under the glass and at the back of the hall. Since dwarves are natural miners, it was appropriate to use an excess of gold and iron.

TIPS TO TAKE FROM THIS BUILD:
Lava can provide a warm light source underground and create a sense of atmosphere.

↗

WARNING: If you're attempting something similar to this, add the lava last. It's very easy to accidentally set yourself, or any flammable blocks, on fire. Always keep a water bucket in your hotbar to deal with any emergencies.

TNT

PALACE BY FYREUK

This magnificent palace building was created using a variety of blocks to give a sense of opulence. You feel like royalty the moment you step inside.

This build shares many similarities with the Dwarven City, with the royal throne at the center and seating on either side. The regal colors of gold and red dominate the color scheme and an excess of gold is used in the main floor and wall designs. An elaborate glowstone lamp sits in the center of the ceiling and illuminates the details nicely.

TIPS TO TAKE FROM THIS BUILD:
Get creative with glowstone to make beautiful indoor lighting, and design interesting floor patterns using colored blocks.

SUSPENSION BRIDGE

The landscape of Minecraft is often littered with dangerous obstacles, from rocky ravines to deep, fast-flowing rivers. The safest and most effective way to overcome these obstacles is to travel over them, so let's build a suspension bridge.

CONSTRUCTION MATERIALS

1

First, build a horizontal strip of wood planks across the obstacle you need to overcome. It should be 2 blocks deep. Make it wide enough to incorporate a minecart track in case you decide to add one later.

2

Build supports underneath the wood planks using wood blocks. Destroy the top layer of central wood planks in the bridge and replace them with gravel. Leave the wood planks in place along the edges.

3

Build an arch under the bridge using wood blocks to match the supports. The arch helps support the bridge but still allows boats to travel underneath it.

4

Add fences along the wood planks at each side of the gravel road, and fill in the space above the arch with fences. Be creative with your fences and try out your own designs.

SUSPENSION BRIDGE
...CONTINUED

et's turn your basic arch bridge into an impressive suspension bridge. Suspension bridges give the impression that they can bear an incredibly heavy load, which is very reassuring to look at!

CONSTRUCTION MATERIALS

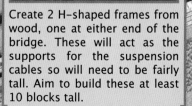

5

Create 2 H-shaped frames from wood, one at either end of the bridge. These will act as the supports for the suspension cables so will need to be fairly tall. Aim to build these at least 10 blocks tall.

6

Create 2 half arches starting at either end of the bridge and meeting in the middle. These represent the large cables that often arch across bridges. To stagger the arch, start with 3 or 4 blocks in a line, then continue dropping them down.

Add fences underneath your arches. You can experiment with patterns or just opt for a simple line effect by spacing your fences a block apart, as we have done. The lines run down to the fences below, so that everything is connected.

Extend your cable pattern to the other sides of the frames back on land to finish it off. You might want to add torches or glowstone lamps. You could also add road markings and paths to the bridge, if your design is wide enough.

TOWER BRIDGE BY GEROO

Recognize this iconic London landmark? Yes, that's right — it's a re-creation of the famous Tower Bridge and was created by Minecrafter Geroo.

Constructed mainly from cobblestone, smooth stone, and stone brick, the bridge towers over everyone and everything in the surrounding area. There are a lot of details to look at, and the use of wool to accent the sides of the bridge is particularly effective. Geroo used the classic Union Jack colors to give the bridge a really British feel. A bridge of this scale would take weeks to build, but it would be worth the effort just to see your friends' jaws drop!

TIPS TO TAKE FROM THIS BUILD:
Take inspiration from real-life structures and re-create them in Minecraft.

MAGE BRIDGE
BY FYREUK

The majority of this fantasy-style bridge is built from stone slabs and cobblestone, and the bridge walkway is fairly simple, but what makes it stand out are the three intricately designed gatehouses.

These gatehouses are multilayered, highly detailed creations. In between them are small stages with mystical mage statues sitting on top of them. It took a team of 20 people just an hour to build this bridge, which is incredible! If you want to create something similar yourself, make sure you set aside a few days to complete it.

A towering mage statue watching over the bridge.

TIPS TO TAKE FROM THIS BUILD:

A bridge can be more than just a bridge — build detailed features into it where you can.

STAINED-GLASS POPPY

There are many ways to bring a splash of color to your builds. Since 1.7.2, you can now create beautiful stained-glass windows. Let's build a stained-glass flower with a Minecraft twist.

1

Build a cobblestone frame. A 19x13 rectangle ensures you have enough space to create a detailed image. Lay out the pattern using wool blocks first; the design will be clearer and, if you make a mistake in Survival mode, you won't have to destroy your precious glass blocks. The stem is 9 blocks tall, and the center of the poppy is 2 blocks and is surrounded by 17 red blocks.

2

Once you're happy with your wool layout, replace the wool with stained-glass. Just remove 1 block at a time and substitute it with the equivalent-colored stained-glass block. Once complete you'll have a transparent version of your wool model.

3

Fill in the remaining empty blocks with regular glass. Presumably your window will be part of a building, and your flower will be a beautiful feature for your chosen room. Stained-glass windows are a relatively new concept, so this is sure to dazzle your friends.

STAINED-GLASS PATTERN

So you've mastered the art of the basic stained-glass window. Let's look at a modern take on a traditional stained-glass window and create a more complex, multicolored pattern.

CONSTRUCTION MATERIALS

1

You'll need to build a large rectangular cobblestone frame. The example here is 18x36 blocks, which is ideal. Find the center of the frame and begin to build outward, copying the shapes of this geometric design (remember to use wool blocks).

2

Once you're happy with the design, replace the wool with stained-glass, as you did for the small stained-glass window. With any luck, the shapes in the pattern will be symmetrical and the overall design will look pretty impressive.

Now fill in the empty blocks with regular clear glass, and your window is finished. This would make a dramatic feature for a larger room or build, such as a banquet hall in a castle.

FAYFALL FANTASY PORT
BY NECKWARE

This colorful fantasy island was built by Neckware and his friend Nemleous. The overall design is simple, but the aesthetic choices — from the variance in color to the powerful sky pattern — make for a truly eye-catching build.

Rather than just using stained-glass to bring a splash of color to the windows, Neckware chose to weave color into all aspects of the build. This level of color can be tough to get right, especially since colored blocks don't come in slab or stair versions, which makes smaller detail more difficult to achieve. The fact that this build looks so elaborate is a testament to the design skill of these builders.

TIPS TO TAKE FROM THIS BUILD:

Be bold and use color throughout your build. With a little thought you can create something truly spectacular.

COLORDREAM
BY DEAD2HUNTER

Dead2hunter has used color in a very interesting way throughout this huge amphitheater-style build, accenting the dark blocks with orange and yellow.

The arches and spikes on the exterior are mirrored in the interior, making this a complex build both from a style and planning perspective.

A multitude of color has been used to break up monotonous flat surfaces both inside and outside. A lot of Minecraft builders shy away from adding color because it can give their builds an unrealistic feel. But, done correctly, accents of color can help create something unique that other Minecrafters will want to replicate.

TIPS TO TAKE FROM THIS BUILD:
Make use of bright, cheerful colors to accent a darker build and break up the large surfaces.

OCEAN TEMPLE

A whole host of underwater-themed blocks were introduced in the 1.8 update. Unsurprisingly, these aqua-colored blocks are ideal for creating ocean-themed structures like temples.

CONSTRUCTION MATERIALS

1

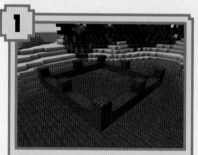

Ideally, this ocean temple should emerge from an ocean or other body of water. Find a suitable spot, then create a dark prismarine base 2 blocks above the surface. This example is an 11x11 block square, with extra blocks to mark the corners and center point of each side.

2

Add a support leg to each corner of the square, extending down as far as necessary to the ocean floor. Now place prismarine brick blocks in between the isolated blocks on top of the square structure to fill in the gaps. Your walls will extend upward from here.

3

Use regular prismarine to create squares on top of the prismarine brick, leaving a 2x2 central square gap in the middle of each. Fill these gaps with cyan stained-glass to create windows. Place 4 sea lanterns behind the glass blocks, then add dark prismarine around the windows and place blocks jutting out at the center and corner points of the top row.

OCEAN TEMPLE

...CONTINUED

CYAN STAINED-GLASS RECIPE

8

You can craft a block of cyan stained-glass from 8 regular glass and 1 piece of cyan dye.

DARK PRISMARINE RECIPE

8

Craft dark prismarine from 8 prismarine shards and an ink sac.

4

Time to build upward. Simply copy the dark prismarine outline from the previous section as many times as you like to create the desired number of floors.

5

Now fill in the rest of the details for the walls and windows on each level. Just repeat the previous steps for the windows and prismarine brick blocks.

Your temple needs a roof to keep the rain out, and will also benefit from a few artistic flourishes to finish it off. A traditional, Japanese-style temple roof will work very well with this build.

6

Stone brick will contrast well with the blues and greens of the temple wall. Use slabs to create small, overhanging details above the windows on each level. This helps break up the design and ensures each level mirrors the overall shape of the temple. You can follow this design or create your own.

7

Create a traditional triangular house roof, but extend the very top layer farther out to create points at the front and back. Get creative and add accents that taper off along the sides. Fill in the triangular space under the roof with extra prismarine and prismarine brick blocks.

8

Your temple needs a point of entry so you can get inside and explore. Try removing 2 of the windowed wall sections and create a 3-block-wide doorway in the center of one side of the temple. Create a dramatic border for the door using dark prismarine and build a staircase leading up to the door out of stone brick and dark prismarine.

SEA TEMPLE
BY XYLIA

Xylia's elaborate sea temple captures the essence of the Minecraft ocean without the help of any ocean-themed blocks. White quartz blocks have been used to accent the aqua-blue tones of the water that the temple sits in, and ice blocks have been used to create blue details that make the whole temple pop.

When building something similar yourself, remember to take height into consideration, particularly if you want your temple to sit on the ocean floor and be completely submerged. Of course, you can also deliberately create a structure like this one, which towers over the ocean.

 TIPS TO TAKE FROM THIS BUILD:
You can create ocean-themed builds without ocean-themed blocks. Don't be afraid to use your imagination!

ATLANTIS BY NINAMAN

This enormous city is inspired by the legend of the submerged city of Atlantis. Rather than being completely underwater, the city is surrounded by a wall to keep the ocean at bay.

The disc-shaped objects in the sky are magical runes made from ice blocks that work well with the circular design of the build overall and add an interesting element of fantasy. Ninaman even nods to science-fiction with the addition of the space fighter-style planes and floating islands scattered across the skies. The staggering level of detail explains why the build took over two months to complete.

TIPS TO TAKE FROM THIS BUILD:

A twist on a classic theme can produce something truly impressive.

FLOATING ISLAND

Floating islands can really add a touch of fantasy to your world and they're great if you're working with a steampunk theme (see page 72). They aren't as complicated as they look, either!

CONSTRUCTION MATERIALS

1

Build a 1x1 cobblestone tower upward, 30–40 blocks tall. This is the center of your island and will eventually be destroyed. At the top of this tower, place cobblestone blocks in a cross, approximately 15 blocks out from the center in each direction. Run a circle of blocks around the cross to create the shape of the island.

2

Start at the edge and add blocks below the top of the island, working in toward the center. The more randomly they are placed, the more realistic your floating island will appear. The four lines of blocks should meet roughly in the middle of your island. Now fill in the top layer of your island with more cobblestone blocks.

3

Here comes the tricky part: sculpting the bottom of the island. Think of each layer as a disc, and try to keep the discs true to the shape of the island, curving them in as you get to the bottom. Continue to do this until you have a shape you are happy with.

4

Add a base layer of grass blocks to the top, then build up 1 or 2 more layers and add trees and flowers. Try to make the layers reflect the shape of the island. Finally, destroy the bottom of the initial block tower so your island floats in the sky.

FLOATING ISLAND
...CONTINUED

What floating fantasy island would be complete without a castle? When you're visiting your floating island, you'll need somewhere to hang out (and keep a lookout for enemies).

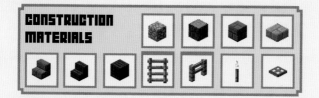
1

First, mark out the basic outline of your castle using cobblestone blocks. Mark out any lookout towers and space for a gate.

2

Raise the walls and towers to your desired height. Our walls are 5 blocks tall, and the towers 8 blocks tall.

FLOATING ISLAND
...CONTINUED

3

Use wood planks to create floors for your towers, with trapdoors and ladders built into them for access. Add wood blocks to each corner of the towers and stone bricks to the tops of the cobblestone walls to reinforce your lookout posts.

4

Build a roof on top of each tower — we used spruce wood stair blocks to create ours. Now add wood planks on top of the walls to create battlements. Try using stone half slabs or stair blocks to change the shape of the build.

MAGE TOWER ISLANDS
BY NEFASHUS

This is part of a collection of carefully planned islands. Each one is packed with small details that together create an awesome scene, but the focal point is the mage tower that you can see here.

Notice the rock formation underneath the islands — along with the waterfall, the jagged outline helps to create a sense of height. The backdrop for your build is equally as important as the build itself. This relatively simple tower looks all the more impressive atop a floating island.

TIPS TO TAKE FROM THIS BUILD:

Location, location, location! Picking the right spot for your build can make the difference between mediocre and outstanding.

STEAMPUNK CITY
BY FYREUK

Steampunk City is FyreUK's biggest floating island build, and what you can see here is just a small section of it. Steampunk is a type of science fiction that features steam-powered machinery.

In keeping with steampunk style, lots of giant propellers have been used to illustrate how the islands are kept afloat. Along with the flying ships, buildings, and balloons, one of the standout features of this build is the large monorail track encircling it. This acts as a tour path, allowing visitors to travel around the islands to see all the different areas.

SHOP

TIPS TO TAKE FROM THIS BUILD:

Think through each detail of your creation to make sure it fits with your theme, and try to add a mode of transport to larger builds so you can give people guided tours and show off all your hard work.

GALLEON SHIP

There are many vast oceans to conquer in Minecraft, and what better way to show you're king of the seas than by building an amazing ship? Assuming you're ready for the challenge, that is . . .

CONSTRUCTION MATERIALS

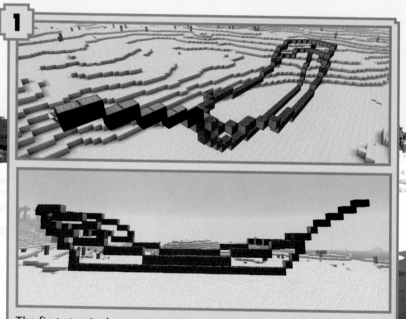

The first step is the most complex; you'll need to create the outline for your ship in your chosen block. This outline will eventually form the hull. Use these images as a guide, but don't feel that you have to copy them exactly. If you want to try a different shape or build something much larger or smaller, go for it!

TIP: This ship was built floating over sand so you can see the detail more clearly, but you can follow this step-by-step and build your ship straight into the ocean.

2

Next, fill in the outline to create the full shape of the ship's hull. We used birch wood planks, since they contrast well with the wood used to create the skeleton of the ship. Stone brick has been used to define the top edges of the hull.

3

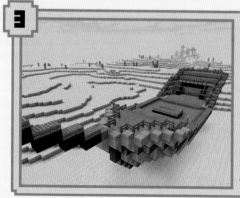

Now fill in the top of the base to form your deck. This deck has a raised section at the back (known as a poop deck), so we added wooden stair blocks along either side of the ship to provide access points. There's also a raised section at the front, and we've added stair blocks there, too, to give the deck a variety of levels.

4

A ship of this size would need plenty of large sails, so construct 3 tall masts out of wood. Make sure you space them out evenly across the deck to make them look realistic. If you build a smaller boat, you won't need as many masts.

CONSTRUCTING THE SAILS

CONSTRUCTION MATERIALS

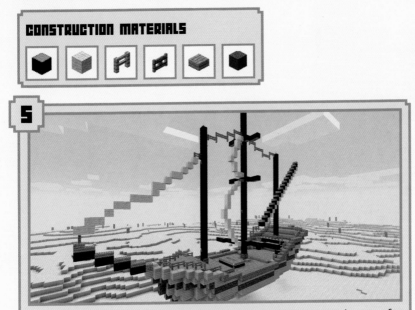

5

Sails can be tricky to master, so make sure you leave enough room for experimentation and enough time for redesigning. We'll be creating 2 large sails in the middle with 2 triangular side sails at the back and front of the ship. Outline each sail now using white wool blocks.

GALLEON SHIP ...CONTINUED

6

Fill in the front and back sails first to get a sense of size and color. We used white wool for the sails and wooden fences to link the masts together. Try to arrange the sail blocks in different layers to make it look as if the wind is blowing behind them.

7

Build 2 front-facing sails in the middle of the ship. We created 3 different types of sail to show you how they can all work together, but you can stick with just 1 if you prefer.

RED WOOL RECIPE

Craft 1 block of red wool from 1 block of wool and rose red dye.

We added flags made out of red wool to the tops of the masts. These also appear to be blowing in the wind. We created a few smaller sails in between the larger sails to give the ship more detail.

COMMUNITY CREATIONS
THE MOST IMPRESSIVE SHIPS ON THE SEVEN SEAS!

MAGE SHIPS
BY FYREUK

These mage ships were built by FyreUK as part of the Mage City. The sails have been created in different ways to give a more elegant, majestic feel to these vessels.

TIPS TO TAKE FROM THIS BUILD:

Experiment with sail design — it'll really make a difference to the overall look of your ship.

While these ships still use wood for the hull and white wool for the sails, the main difference is the triangular side sails that span the entire length of the ship. Three of these sails stretch along the ship and create a very different look from other ships of similar scale and style.

PIRATE ISLAND SHIP
BY HEAVEN_LORD

Minecrafter Heaven_Lord and his team created a huge Pirate Island with various ships of different sizes and styles. This is one of the ships found in the waters around Pirate Island.

The hull was built out of yellow and black wool as an interesting alternative to the standard brown wooden hulls we're so used to seeing for ships of this scale. The addition of small cannons along the side of the hull is another interesting detail. The huge sails give the ship a grand scale, ensuring it towers over the ocean waves below.

TIPS TO TAKE FROM THIS BUILD:
Go back to old builds and improve them with additional features like cannons.

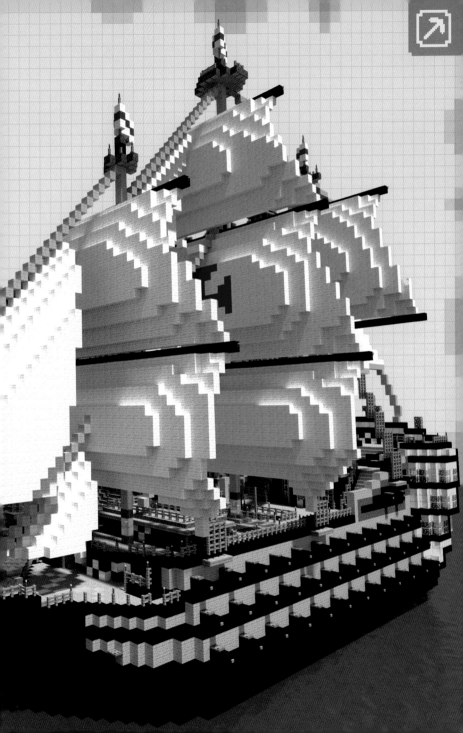

EPIC ROLLER COASTER

Why not turn a regular method of transport into a twisting, turning, plummeting roller-coaster ride? Here's how to construct the basics. Where you go after that is up to you!

CONSTRUCTION MATERIALS

TIP: To start and stop minecarts and to propel them uphill, you'll need powered rails. They'll need a power source to work, which can be supplied by a redstone torch, a detector rail, a lever, a button, or another circuit.

RAILS RECIPE 16

You can craft 16 rails from 6 iron ingots and 1 stick.

POWERED RAILS RECIPE 6

You can craft 6 powered rails from 6 gold ingots, 1 stick, and 1 redstone.

1

Create an outline for your track using wood planks. You'll need a few drops to give the cart the momentum it needs to travel around the track, and twists and turns to create a fun ride. Position your rails on top of the wood planks. Place powered rails at the bottom of the first climb and keep testing your roller coaster until the cart can make it to the top.

EPIC ROLLER COASTER

...CONTINUED

2

Add more detail. We placed a tunnel at the end of our ride to add another level of excitement. There's nothing quite like careening around tight corners in the dark! We also built supports underneath the track, using fence blocks for the struts, to make it look realistic.

3

Add stair blocks to the side of the track where it runs uphill to give it an authentic look. Pick a point on a flat section to create a minecart station, which you can use as your start/finish ride point. Add a dispenser full of minecarts here.

4

Add glowstone lamps around your ride to illuminate it at night, and a fence to stop mobs wandering onto the track. Finally, add some trees, grass, and flowers around the outside of the fence and on top of your tunnel so that it blends in with the landscape.

DISPENSER RECIPE

You can craft a dispenser from 7 blocks of cobblestone, 1 bow, and 1 redstone.

MINECART RECIPE

You can craft a minecart from 5 iron ingots.

EPIC ROLLER COASTER
ADVANCED FEATURES

What's that? Already bored of your basic track, you say? Okay, you asked for it: Let's look at adding some even more awesome features to your ride to make it a really nail-biting experience!

MULTIPLE DAREDEVIL DROPS

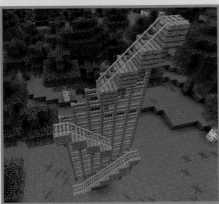

Add daredevil drops to your track to make your roller coaster even more exciting. To create a drop, let your minecart fall off 1 track and onto another track below, and repeat as many times as you like. You can change direction as you go, but you'll need to ensure the lower track is directly below the upper so that the cart doesn't miss, otherwise your friends may sue you for injury!

HALF-PIPE DESIGN

Try a half-pipe design and send your minecart along a snaking track. To keep the cart moving, place booster rails at the bottom of each dip. You can make your snaking track as long or as short as you like, depending on how many turns you think your stomach can handle!

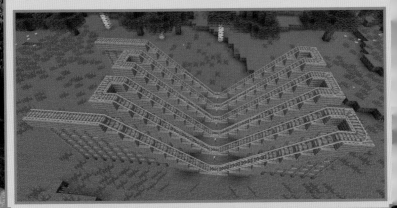

RED DRAGON COASTER
BY CRESPOCHIMP

This terrifying roller coaster built in and around a valley has been designed to look like a dragon. The ride starts at the head, then twists and turns its way down the body.

You'll notice a distinct lack of support structures for this ride, which adds to the unsteady, dangerous feeling. The minecart is constantly careening around corners at top speed, and the view is absolutely petrifying. CrespoChimp used the natural terrain of the ravine, dropping down into the caves and then shooting into the sky.

TIPS TO TAKE FROM THIS BUILD:
Use the natural terrain to its full potential by dipping and soaring around its features.

NO ESCAPE
BY IHDVIBE22

o Escape was created using a handful of simple roller coaster features mixed in with some more complex ones. The builder combines them all in clever ways to create a truly thrilling ride.

When the ride begins you're dropped onto the track below by pistons. The majority of the track is supported by 1-block-wide pillars, creating that rickety impression again as well as an open feel. This is an unpredictable ride that will keep you guessing at every turn.

TIPS TO TAKE FROM THIS BUILD:

Removing roller coaster supports opens up the entire build as well as giving it a dangerous feel.

FINAL WORDS FROM FYREUK

Congratulations! You've made it to the end of the Minecraft Construction Handbook, which means you're a master builder of the highest order.

FyreUK are constantly being asked for their Number One construction tip, and the reply is usually to focus on detail and add it to your builds wherever possible. Create patterns and use different blocks to break up large sections such as walls and roofs to give your builds more depth and make them more realistic. Don't be afraid to be creative!

USEFUL LINKS

Check out this list of useful websites. They'll really extend your Minecrafting experience.

Official Minecraft website:
https://minecraft.net

Official Mojang website:
https://mojang.com

The Minecraft wiki:
www.minecraftwiki.net

The official Facebook page:
www.facebook.com/minecraft

Mojang Team's YouTube channel:
www.youtube.com/teammojang

The official Minecraft Twitter page:
https://twitter.com/Mojang

Jeb's official Twitter page:
https://twitter.com/jeb_

Here are some other Minecraft sites, not monitored by Mojang or Scholastic. Enter at your own risk!

Detailed server information:
minecraftservers.net

Texture packs:
www.minecrafttexturepacks.com

Minecraft on Reddit:
www.reddit.com/r/Minecraft/

FyreUK's YouTube channel:
www.youtube.com/fyreuk

(See page 6 for our "Stay Safe Online" policy.)